Up, Out & Over

Up, Out & Over

Poems by

Jack Mackey

© 2024 Jack Mackey. All rights reserved.
This material may not be reproduced in any form, published,
reprinted, recorded, performed, broadcast,
rewritten, or redistributed without
the explicit permission of Jack Mackey.
All such actions are strictly prohibited by law.

Cover design by Shay Culligan
Cover photo by Bradley Weaver
Author photo by Bradley Weaver

ISBN: 978-1-63980-629-4
Library of Congress Control Number: 2024943455

Kelsay Books
502 South 1040 East, A-119
American Fork, Utah 84003
Kelsaybooks.com

For My Children

and

Brad, of course

Acknowledgments

Versions of some of these poems were published previously in the following journals. My sincere thanks to the editors.

Anti-Heroin Chic: "Gravity Keeps the Moon in Orbit"
Bay to Ocean (Eastern Shore Writer's Association): "Pandemic Blues Day 43: In Which I Invite the Germs In," "Lingering Questions"
Broadkill Review: "Why It Took Odysseus Ten Years to Get Home," "Apologies to the Bus Driver Fifty Years Too Late"
Compassionate Friends (We Need Not Walk Alone): "Now I Run Alone"
Darkhouse Books: "A Guardrail" (*Descansos*), "Today I Bought New Cutlery" (*What We Talk About When We Talk About It, Vol. 2*)
Gargoyle: "The History of Rock & Roll," "Hamartia," "When You Wish You Were Still Stupid," "Ada Limon Perches on My Knee and Reads Her Poems," "Happy Endings," "The History of Rock & Roll"
Impostor: "Reason No.1001"
In Parenthesis: "Missing Pieces," "Only Humans Know They Will Die"
Mobius: "We Promised"
Mojave River Review: "A Poetic Biography"
Panoply: "This Flag is Not Waving"
Rat's Ass Review: "Undercharged"
Rehoboth Beach Writer's Guild (Scenes: A Collaboration of Coastal Writers and Artists): "Once Again the Flock"
Third Wednesday: "Changing Trains in Jamaica," "The Harbor Finally"
Writers Resist: "The President Signs the Criminal Justice Reform Act"

Contents

UP

How to Catch a Ball	15
God's Eye	17
Our Last Lunch	18
Happy Endings	20
Holes	21
The Harbor, Finally	23
The Chemistry of Fusion	24
In Which I Have Unlimited Choices and My Sister Has One	25

OVER

Luray, Virginia	29
The 1701 Q Street Commitment	31
Vietnam, 1973	32
Undercharged	33
How I Became a Superhero	34
Why It Took Odysseus Ten Years to Get Home	36
Today I Bought New Cutlery	38
The Receipt	40
Ode to a Basketball	41
Right Way/Wrong Way/Anyway or Why I Stopped Shouting Orders	43

OVER (Again)

I Can Still Hear It	47
That Christmas in California	49

The Last Thing to Go	50
Only Humans Know They Will Die	51
Neverland	53
A Guardrail	54
Missing Pieces	55
Air BnB in the Subjunctive	56
Gravity Keeps the Moon in Orbit	57
When You Really Wish You Were Still Stupid	59
Now I Run Alone	60

OUT

Changing Trains in Jamaica	63
Lingering Questions	65
The Night My Mother and I Killed a Bottle of Scotch	67
The Bachelorette Party Lands in a Gay Bar	69
Reason No. 1001	70

MOREOVER

It's Funny How You Remember Stuff	73
I Announce to an Empty Room I'm Going for a Walk	75
Be Careful	77
Disproving a Negative	78
Knock, Knock, Knockin'	79
Apologies to the Bus Driver Fifty Years Too Late	80
Tied	81
The Load Uncarried	82

These Houses Are Too Close	84
Discovery	86

OTHER

A Poetic Biography	89
Ada Limon Perches on My Knee and Reads Her Poems	90
Hamartia	92
Once Again, the Flock	93
SAD	94
The History of Rock & Roll	95
Pandemic Blues Day 43: In Which I Invite the Germs In	96
How to Draw a Line Without a Pencil	97
The President Signs the Criminal Justice Reform Act	99
This Flag Is Not Waving	100
We Promised	101

UP

How to Catch a Ball

Sunday afternoon, the April sun
higher in the sky, burning into
Barnes & Noble's windows,
I'm inside, a respite from heartlessness,
fed up with the unceasing heat
beating on Florida cement,
outside a scene pock-marked by
weekend walkers scrolling screens
in their hands or listening to thrillers
through plugs in their languid ears,
I'm here to get something
I can't quite label,
to fill the cavern in my head,
dried out from salty water, sunscreen
and book bans,
passing YA lit
the how-to's, a latte station,
I find the down escalator and finally
the fiction: three shelves of titles
hidden in the low-profit catacombs
behind the books-on-disc.

My father on the end of the couch,
a baseball game on mute,
reading lamp glowing over
his shoulder and half a ginger
snap in his mouth,
devouring a library book
or one from the second-hand store
he maybe already read, or not,
one always open on his lap
no matter if the Yankees
were ahead, leans forward,

his half-sleeved arm illuminated
& says Look, extending
to me across the room,
Read this page, it's beautiful,
hoping somewhere in the future—
because it's not happening
while I'm twelve—
I'll bite,
neither of us suspecting
one day I'll call home
to announce I'm
graduating or, in a bookstore
on some distant Sunday, I'll pay
full price for Toni Morrison.

God's Eye

I began to lose my faith when my mother
got a new clothesline—one hand shading
her eyes, the other holding the aluminum arm
of the contraption whose pole
my father cemented in the yard,

a pinwheel of damp clothes entwined,
its arms strapped together by
laminated cord, waving faded dungarees,
emerald school uniforms,
a torn red flannel shirt, worn on its third brother,
flapping in time to somebody's definition
of rhythm, like a woven eye, lying on its side
circling the pole & spinning,
she stared up at a threatening sky.

The Mormon mother of ten down
the street smiled at us, she could afford
to smile, with a dryer in her basement,
never fretted over weather.

My mother washed two loads a day
forever, the storm arriving
despite her plans, demanding
she put down the latest kid on the closest carpet,
dash madly out the door to unpin
the flapping damp before the sky
would ruin everything, left me asking how

could God's clean rain turn things dirty.

Our Last Lunch

As her hair was turning gray my mother left
New York winters and opened a gift shop in the lobby

of a Chula Vista motel. Time was she'd close
two station wagon doors with her arms

full of groceries, now she had a pick-up
with a stick shift and didn't need a lesson. It all

came back to her, the girl she was, the fun, and
the pleasure of meeting someone with a backstory.

When I showed up one day without
calling, I watched her for a long time

through the lobby glass—her easy way
with people, carefully folding a dreamcatcher

in tissue paper like it was going to her own
grandchild. I appeared, she turned

around the OPEN sign, stepped into the hall,
and locked the door. Bifocaled, her hair flecked

with white, she led me by the hand
to the motel café. Once she signed my school

reports, muttered about the future, now the future
had arrived and here I was. We floated

above our table, spoke in weathered tones, shared
a sandwich, overlapped, again, our hands.

The afternoon bowed out, shadows crept in lazy
steps across the café wall. Her eyes turned to

the cloudy window, my hazy face flashed in her glasses,
I looked past her as the CLOSED sign slipped

its hook, gently slid down the glass to the floor.

Happy Endings

Today our neighbors
removed a fence we thought
we shared,
we believed it
right on the line, not theirs
or ours, so tonight the dog got lost,
the faithful scents
gone, stars behind clouds &
moon covered over,
making the search for her more dire,
no border to orient
our eyes.
The hour was a week, it seemed,
our girl so old
the cold so resolute
we were sure she couldn't endure.
We found her cowered in a corner
waiting to fall asleep.

When my father had had enough—
the tumor lodged
between his ribs, walking impossible
even talking painful—
we carried him
my brothers and I,
positioned him
in a comfortable spot in the sun,
a warm place, familiar
walls and pictures, to look
past the open windows
drink in the jasmine
take the pills
and wait.

Holes

Like me my father
planted tomatoes but
I don't remember it. Instead
I picture him mixing plaster
in a Maxwell House can,
a trowel in his stoic hand, layering
white pasty filling into
a hole in their bedroom wall,

a string holding something in place
something unseen,
hanging from the space
he'd filled before, too many times
because his wife, my mother,
awakened on weekend mornings
from her groggy sleep
by the screaming kids
she couldn't stop

from fighting over which cartoon
to watch, she'd flung
the door open with such force
the ceramic knob whacking the wall,
broke the plaster
and landed once again
inside the sheetrock like a fist.
He never said a word.

This memory returns
on a cold day in mid-May
as I make
small depressions in the dirt
with two fingers,

place seedlings in the holes
& brush loose soil
over their roots, where they'll struggle
in the sweltering summer
that lays down hard on this city.

By mid-August I'll get payback
in fruit, so my father will say
again in my head,
That was worth it.

The Harbor, Finally

My sisters wheeled
my father's bed into the living room so
he could feel the sun, look out, watch the seaside golfers
drive long balls into the blue and drop
into the fairway of mounding jade waves.

Bit by bit he was slipping,
releasing the grip on his anger at all of us
and my mother, who seized the wheel years ago
steering to a swell of monthly worries,
aging hospital bills, holy books,
and canceled tee times. He accepted
how his course was mapped by rhythmic tides
and sermons from the unknowing.

Now my mother rested by his bed,
her constant hand lying on his,
holding the pulsing ache of the years, gazing
past his fading eyes, out to the green sea.

He finally understood
these accidental adults in this worn out house,
our whispered laughs echoing summer swims,
here by choice, thanking him, controlling our goodbyes,
plunging into the necessary, as we
swabbed our family vessel, filling the hull with reconciliation,
sweeping over the bow decades of
dredged-up golf balls and counterweights.

The Chemistry of Fusion

A sweet spring morning
we restart our interrupted dreams,
clutching vessels
from my sister's safekeeping:
ersatz urns, ziplocked plastic baggies;
our bare hands scoop, unclench
our fists, toss skyward as freeing a bird
their incense-infused triturate,
parents co-mingled,
taken by breezy sunlit spirals &
wafting through air saturated in magnolia,
over this park, this extended backyard
behind the house we left behind,
recalling our childhood
hopes and disappointments,
some landing on our shoes, then whooshed away
onto sparse blades, exposing
empty fingers and belated gratitude.

The photo snapped, the grandchildren
comforted, a generation returned
to the earth, we fly away,
the music done,
the reason for convening resolved,
the next reunion
for one of us.

In Which I Have Unlimited Choices and My Sister Has One

Early, on the cool linoleum foyer floor,
a coloring book of mazes and a box of crayons—
countless combinations in front of me.

The front door opened and my mother
carried in my last sister, the one who would
never carry a baby to term, never have
any regrets, stepping over my boy's torso
sprawled out, as my father said Watch
your step and pointed.

Above, later, a grey-brown cluster of twigs
barely balanced in the portico, an evolution
of maternal choice, a million trials and turns
of innate perfection, where she nestled,
her belly warming shells of blazing blue.

Below, later still, on the ground a broken
thing fluttered abandoned perhaps, or perhaps
too eager to fly and a child asking what
to do. I considered just flinging it away
or using my boot. I answered with a gloved
hand, a bucket of water, a lesson in mercy.

OVER

Luray, Virginia

Blue Ridge maples
unfurling in oranges and reds
against a lay-low sky in the rear mirror,
my soon-to-be-wife—three months
into it, just a bump—checks the map
& I steer us towards the caverns.

The bend of a carved-out trail,
we walk into quiet dark
almost pitch,
all underneath-ness, giving way to
tiny lights flickering like new stars,
a sonorous tour master echoes the history—
a lost Indian boy's bones,
prehistoric teeth found only a few years ago,

the whole hollow carved by accident,
no one suspecting for eons
as they walked above,
its shallow pools reflect
a ceiling of rich umber,
dripping into rusty green-blue striations,
oozing for a million years,
a porous miracle produced from inside out.

She seems interested enough in the tour,
a real trooper with all the walking and standing,
I catch for the first time
her unconscious hand moving
under a crocheted poncho to her belly,
as she steps over a puddle or
ducks under a stalactite.

She's unaware,
both of us feeling our way,
gripping hard the handrails.

The 1701 Q Street Commitment

Cornered in the Dupont Circle neighborhood
that mutated from Hippie Haven to Gay Central,
nestled among homes of once-illustrious families
broken into pieces and sold separately,
the building morphed from Planned Parenthood
clinic in the 80's to real estate office today.

In those bygone days one monthly night
they'd unlock the front door for men—a handful
of us that night, and adjust the
stirrups for heavier legs,
open the back door to a suburban doctor
who snipped away through evening hours,
disconnecting wish from bone, Russian
from roulette, leaving us a little less, but better.
Three months after the fourth one came out kicking
sense into my wavering head, I stepped up,
lay back, inhaled the icy air of regret and relief—
nothing would be left to chance again . . .

all of which made for a strange exchange
last week, with the fresh-faced lawyer, his head
down, passing
papers for my wobbly signature, requiring
a new commitment—a mortgage for longer
than it takes to raise a kid—longer than
I'll probably be around. Too young to 've seen
what the sea can do, oblivious to the passages
a building goes through—and people. He thought
they created this office for him last year.

I decided to bring him up to date, stopped
signing for just a second and said
I was in this same room 20 years ago,
& waited for him to ask.

Vietnam, 1973

2 a.m. summer, tables mostly cleaned, floors
cleared just barely, like a minefield,
a motley party of young men
with unclipped black bowties in our pockets,
starched and bleached boleros now a sweat-stained
pile left for laundry outside the restaurant door.

Thirsty to beat curfew we rushed to the only bar
still serving, around the pool table, racked and
re-racked colored balls, knocked back whisky in glass
jars. The war raged on without us—lottery-lucky
or too old, or just too worn down, we didn't fight,
we didn't consider ourselves lucky but should've.

I walked home half asleep, tried to imagine what
I would have done, where I would have gone,
or run, too invested in this new family
to swallow the risk.

Coins heavy in my pockets I drooped through
summer vapor, moonlit midges swarming, gassy
asphalt stank sweet of motor oil, rubber stains and
sweat ran down the middle of the street, like a tank
plowed through it mere minutes ago, in the ghostly
quiet, my unsteady cadence of footsteps
tapping to the bed you waited in, asleep, where
we made love and you didn't wake up.

Undercharged

Under the burning glare of
fluorescent lights
of the ice cream shop
on a steamy summer vacation night,
I cheated the man
out of a dollar or so,
wordlessly accepting the change
in my palm,
when, our eyes meeting, you saw
the look on my face.

You looked up at me,
saying nothing,
studying something.

What did you learn when,
as soon as you got outside,
your scoop hit
the pavement with a plop,
your eyes spurted tears
with instant disappointment,
and we went back inside
to the same man
who gave you
another one
for free?

How I Became a Superhero

Leaning low, the vet said Henry,
the hamster, was probably already old
when Santa left him. No surprise then
that night, curling himself into
a furry-round, dirty-brown ball,
expired early in his cage before
my daughter awoke.
Never made it to Easter.

Good Friday and
a furtive, five a.m. burial,
I took her little hand in mine after breakfast,
stepped to a moist brown mound
of overturned earth. A good time
for a lesson: Yes, everyone does,
yes, but not for a very
very long time, nothing
to worry about now.

What lesson then when
I drove up later
and she led me by the hand
to that same spot? *Daddy, look!*
There he sat, nose twitching, on top
of a freshly dug tunnel, looking around
then staring straight at me
as if to say *Really?*

Really, I then remembered—
hamsters burrow, that is, *live*
hamsters burrow. Thinking quick,
I marveled aloud how
my magic had worked,

stifling further life lessons and
the resurrection metaphor that was
begging to be released.

When he died for good
a few weeks later, I rolled
him in a ball of fluorescent green
Easter grass, hurled him
into the woods, said he ran away,
glanced nervously out the window.

Why It Took Odysseus Ten Years to Get Home

We walk around the weekly farmer's market booths, bleached sails
billowing in the breezes of June, light flitting onto tables, white
    linen
unfurling like water lilies, glittering bottles of blackberry jam and
    plates
of peach slices oozing nectar. No one in a hurry, no one in need.
We taste, make a lunch of samples, crab cakes, a handful of
    popcorn.
Tapping guitar strings try to recreate the 60's, the pulpy ballads
    now
squeezed dry of memories. A tepid siren in the distance, but no
heads move. The afternoon slides gently away like a receding
wave, drawing into itself the stillness of the air, the sun-soaked
    metaphors
of completeness and a lack of care. I can't think of anything
we still need, so why am I so hungry?

I sneak away to the car and wait for you to finish choosing the
    perfect corn,
I tidy up the mess, the backlog of half-busy lives. Papers on the
    floor
reveal the recent weeks, mail opened, placed back into envelopes
    and
discarded, the receipts from the auto repair, wine store, thrift shop,
    doctors.
I spread them out on my lap, press out the wrinkles, promise
    myself
to deal with them later.

Waiting for your return I stare at the passenger seat, I want to reach
across and squeeze your hand, lead your peach-juice fingers to my
    mouth.
Suddenly you appear, your arms full of green and silk, I pick up
    the pile
of receipts so you can sit down.
We are on a voyage, it seems, well-provisioned, a hull full
of overdue notices, heavy with the weight of hollow cravings.
Under cloud-covered stars we float, hold outdated charts and scan
    the horizon,
take turns at the rudder, skim past whirlpools and monsters, and arc
into currents circling the rocks.

Today I Bought New Cutlery

a whole set
to replace the crap I bought when I first moved out.
It reminded me of the time we bought
our first knives and forks and spoons,
two of each, all we needed
for that upstairs furnished flat
with ratty carpet and cockroaches.
I think we went to Woolworths
in some rundown strip mall outside D.C.,
on a rainy Friday night in mid-September,
after our passion had burst through spring
and flattened summer,
oblivious then to loan payments and slow leaking tires,
now we had real dinner times to consider.
We had decided to settle in for a while,
clutching our recent sheepskins and
carrying our casual first creation, beating quietly.

Earlier in the day, I carried out the trash
that contained plastic, paper, crystal, silver,
I uncovered the new diary you gave me that I did not
keep, would not keep,
that I had forgotten, lying
still secure in its blankness in the dumpster, longing
to be forgotten again,
to be re-covered, deep, in a landfill.

I found the spoon we used to make instant coffee,
all we ever drank for years,
never committing the time to brew anything.
I have a small scar over my eye from the fork,
the bent one you threw at me
on the cluttered night when I told you.

After I left we had to find a way
to bury the past without burying everything.
When I see you now
your face shines with the pain of what we lost—
the heart we thought would thump forever—
and the sorrow of eating alone.

The Receipt

In May the call came, your echoing voice
lifting the fog of all those years now gone,
introducing yourself as if
I would no longer know
the voice that beguiled me in chemistry class.
Where was it, did I have it,
the receipt for the plot we bought
back when we planned deep for the future—
an unmarked piece of grass shadowed
between your mother and the sun.
New cemetery owners and records lost you said,
you had an immediate need, for your sister,
her ending a light you saw coming at you.
I had to remind you I didn't
have it, I left with nothing.

July, after you buried her somewhere
else, my pocket buzzes with a texted photo,
the lost paper, a two-dimensional flicker on flat black,
you want me to see you found it—
proof the parcel is ours still. I can picture the spot,
a smear of green sideways to a mound
of soft sun-dried dirt, all we hoped for
gradually settling, sinking. I texted back
Great news! Happy it can be used some day.

We both knew it would lay there forever,
Yes, hope not too soon LOL,
nothing more to say, edges of
torn-open lives now left to seal again,
the texts trailed off in colorful emojis
slipping, scrolling & disappearing as the screen
dissolved in icons for weather and time.

Ode to a Basketball

O, torturing basketball, wreathed
by lines curving your abrasive cover,
your speckled skin
the color of an orange plucked
from muddy water, in the palm
of Tommy's buoyant hand, the supple
jazz formed from a thousand afternoons,
both of you weightless & rising
to the sky-bleached backboard,
him lifting a mocking offering
to the gods he'd already tamed,
then bounding you against concrete.
Boom!

From the bench I ached
for that—just one basket,
my body lithe, muscled arms right like his,
a steel hoist lifting its weightless freight
in the sun. Damn you, basketball,
I lost faith in you in high school,

but you're bouncing back here
this Saturday morning, I watch
from the stands, sitting with other dads
inside the cafeteria-gym, ten-year-olds
stampede from one end to the other,
dribbling you, trying not to trip,
laying you up or lobbing you
from mid-court,
fouling each other like crazy.

I marvel at how
earnest they are, how my kid handles
you, her confidence, unaware how beautiful
she is, how she, unlike her hapless
parent in the bleachers, handles with ease
whatever bounces her way.

Right Way/Wrong Way/Anyway
or Why I Stopped Shouting Orders

I was fifteen, got a dollar-twenty-five before
taxes every twelve-hour day at the country
club. Betty showed me the right way to hoist a tray

onto my left shoulder, keeping my right hand
free to grab a dirty cup or carry an entree
to a waitress who left it in the kitchen.

Halfway through August they made
it right, raised me to a buck-forty
when I pointed out the new guy got that.

Later a girlfriend pointed out my lop-sided back, how
my muscled left lat stood out, my right shoulder
drooped. I shrugged each time she said it.

In the fall I could buy a school jacket, the kind
with leather sleeves we think of today as jock kit,
which I wasn't, it seemed wrong to swagger when

I couldn't beat anyone on the track team. I quit
but wore it anyway. Anyway I got a varsity
letter for cheerleading, balancing co-eds

high over my head, both hands squeezing
their sneakers. Years later a doctor stared at the
X-rays, mumbled Something's wrong here.

Tonight, leaving a restaurant my daughters are
furious with me but I insist I was right to make
the waiter come around the table to take my order.

OVER (Again)

I Can Still Hear It

Today a dead tree down
the street is being removed,
disposed of, and
some unseen ogre
roars from beneath
the bushes as I drive by,
unseen men in hardhats,
an unmarked white truck
parked, and the howl
of some belching machine-beast eating
whole limbs in single bites,
vomiting up chips, the stench of diesel,
clouds of sawdust spewed then
settling like unburnt, mortified ash
on my azaleas three houses away,
the neighbors on edge with the snarls,
all the roar, the chomps and bellowing,
we wait for the next growl,
wonder will the work stop,
the creature retreat,
the tree be gone, the thunder cease.

I leaned over
put my head down
on the gurney,
on the clean
white sheet,
exhaled a moan
ascending to
a wail I did not
know as my own,

rising from my gut
rising in volume
pushing past the walls
and windowed swinging doors,
startling
everyone in the hallway,
worrying them
I might go next.

That Christmas in California

A month later I ignored the pleadings of my credit card and bought last-minute tickets to where my kids' aunts and uncles had put down roots, where they became parents themselves, our brooding tree spread out like a branch of hot Celtic lightning, subjecting the Angelinos to crackles of Long Island accents and attitude, and where they stayed awake, kept their kids up, sat at the airport or around lighted palm trees, waited for us to land safely, which we did, after five hours in the air, somewhere around midnight, after ignoring caroling back East, after spending a frantic hour looking for long-term parking, after rushing through a quiet terminal, joining late planners, students fresh out of finals, ethnic outliers, and others too spent to do anything for the holidays but lie in the arms of lovers, after we walked into the cleaned-up undersold cavern of a jumbo jet, spread out, settled into separated seats under reading lights dim as campfires on a hillside, after we looked out at the stars and tried to forget that this had shaken us like a 5 a.m. tremor, spilled us out of bed and worked loose our bolts, that we were not whole any more, that nothing would be the same, that the bounding teenage boy who ruined us with his lovely annoyances, his unrelenting ball-bouncing, tongue-clicking, big-sister-teasing grins—was not with us, would never again be with us . . . and we were desperate for family.

The Last Thing to Go

When my aunt said how did you know, I answered
my mother told me, thinking she meant how did
you know he was in the hospital, but she really meant

how did you know he was dying right now. That's how
I was present the first time, not even his sons my cousins
got there in time. My aunt spoke to him, I whispered

something stupid, the nurse assuring us that hearing
is the last sense to go, and I walked my aunt to her car
like it was just a Friday night and went home.

My mother sobbed when I called her, her brother.

The next time I wasn't so surprised, three days we sat
there, getting updates from messengers in green scrubs
we never saw again after their shift, the loud

speakers in the tiled hallways called out for someone
or something throughout the night, echoing
the aloneness of that vigil, except for one nurse who

probably lived nearby and was always there and fresh,
her hair still wet. I caught her crying later, talking to herself,
leaning over & murmuring to him while she washed his body.

I'm sorry, she looked at me, your son

Only Humans Know They Will Die

In the aftermath,
days later,
the old Lab climbed the stairs,
her crooked legs
arthritic and brittle,
ascending levels from basement to
bedroom, wondering—
looking for

the boy
who just the other day
carried her up
and down the stairs, two skinny arms
cradling this hound so heavy with age,
sparing her creaking pain
dawn to dark,
she now bewildered
by the mystery of it
the gone feel of him on her fur
the absent clatter, the din only
a boy can make,
while we, still here,

marveled how
she still picked up his scent
unaware of what happened,
unaware of what would happen,
whispered how we could see
a tomorrow she could not,
knew we would soon
lose her too,

then walked down the hill,
the shovel dropped,
dusting dirt from our hands,
we knew we'd carry
in our weary arms forever
the dense, opaque
weight
of our hollowed-out hope.

Neverland

It's the anniversary and we've hightailed it
away from the reminders to someplace
safe by the sea. After his sisters go to bed,

I unspool the thread I grabbed at the market
& wrestle the wounded umbrella rescued
from the trashcan at the edge of the beach.

I carefully sew the canopy material back
to the twisted ribs, needling new life into
what's left, re-attaching its thin green shade.

The room is dark, I am alone with a twinkling
light and a coil of yellow, thinking
of the girl sewing the shadow back

on the boy who wouldn't grow up,
his darkened outline never to fade,
hooked as he was on flying forever,

and awake in this rickety beach house
I listen for a window to open.

A Guardrail

If only I had fallen to earth
Hephaestus-like
on shattered legs
even one day earlier,
hobbled
I would have forged
my father's defense
of the strongest steel
before you walked that road.
Instead
today
I paint your name—
where drivers might notice
might slow briefly
might pause—
on this bent and rusted reminder
hammering my blazing brush
in brilliant colors
bellowing your name
into the gale.

Missing Pieces

I look down at my hotel
breakfast as my waiter, in shorts,
unsteady on plastic legs,
tells me he lost both in a fire
at a school of dance he once ran,
says he's not complaining ("I could be
pushing up daisies") and smiles.
I smile back but can't believe he's sincere.
I look down at my phone
the missing face behind cracked glass.

Late afternoon laps, I try to hold on, wonder
can I replace it or should I
continue to limp? Some things have
no plastic equivalents.
I look above & below the water line,
through goggle glass,
the bisected scene in cement and green, a puddle
of grief and memory, and wonder
why does all of it land in your lousy lap
not someone else's, the found twenty staring up
from the pavement, did you deserve it?
the flames? the drowsy driver?

The waiter reappears in a swim suit, slips
off his legs, a blissfully oblivious man who'll
play the ante before he sees his hand,
it's the pleasure of the game that counts,
eases into the pool, into the cool slow
feather-blue, healing dark,
his strokes ignite ripples on the surface,
waltzes like he still has legs.
I swim alongside, study
his dance.

Air BnB in the Subjunctive

I'd like to think you would've been eager to go,
you had that sense of adventure I wished

for, taking after your mother more. You'd've
bugged me to block off weeks, X out

the calendar & keep the renters away
from the pied à terre in Europe your family

now owned. And I'd've complied—
too easily friends would say, giving up

the rental income so my son could sleep
in a bed, bring a girlfriend maybe along, pick

up phrases from the local tongue, walk
the wobbly stones and devour the world

I'd made available to you—an investment
you didn't live to see mature. But that's all

speculation; none of it can happen now.
Instead, I set the Wi-Fi password

to include your name, so South Africans,
Vietnamese, Aussies, Russians—global holiday

goers have to write it down, whisper while
they thumb it into their phones,

with every turnover conjuring you like a séance,
permeating the air with you, the earth with you.

Gravity Keeps the Moon in Orbit

This morning I went back, was lying
on the carpet with you and your sisters
climbing over me, clawing at my shirt,
trying to ride my bucking back, knees digging
into my ribs, elbows and feet flying, the air filled
with giggles and pleas of Give up, Dad
while your mother stirred something the kitchen.

Tonight the earth spins and the moon beams
through the den window, your sisters
are grown, and I write a check
for the one who married
for love, who needs me
a little bit yet, called to drop a hint
(a baseball glove for a grandson),
and I wonder if you'd've called
when a romance dropped and broke
or a job was held beyond
your grasp, or had a son.

Now I sit here holding—
it fits almost perfectly in my palm—
the plaster cast we made
of your warm hand, while you slept,
your sleep not really sleep at all,
before they brought the papers to sign.
Even now I feel your knee,
my hand resting under the sheet.

The cold fingers loose, cupping, closed
enough to hold, but still able to let
moonlight pass
through, and pattern
the light on my lap.

I place the cast back on the bookcase shelf,
slip the check in its envelope,
run my lip along its gluey edge,
walk to the mailbox
and look up.

When You Really Wish You Were Still Stupid

After happy hour, feeling at a loss
I stumble along the boardwalk into
the racket here (it could deafen
a thousand ears—and tonight
it almost does) stand under a beach
town tent, holidays in full tilt, by
the kiddie rides: the carousel, then
little fire trucks and finally
a few feet from mini-boats
afloat in inches of water, moving in
circles, carrying toddler cowboys
fire fighters and sailors,
each looking around to see
a thumbs-up from moms and dads—
you're safe, have fun, I won't
let anything bad happen to you.

I try not to see that horse break
a leg and fall, the fire engine
careen over a cliff, little boats
get sucked into a whirlpool,
I try not to shout Watch Out over the din,
run over and pluck them from peril,
hold their hands, caress their silky heads,
carry them away, I can't but
that doesn't mean I don't need to.

They think they have it all
the parents looking at me funny,
one elbows her husband, nods my way
and now I'm aware I'm a little
too close to them, they sense danger
but have no idea it's not me, they don't
know what I know.

Now I Run Alone

We didn't follow my plan.
At first I heard
the tap-patting of your sneakers next to mine
I slowed us down
teaching, holding
We were supposed to stay together
take it slow
cross the finish line together.
The mile clock blinked our lazy time as we swam
through the dusky mist
through wet evening soggy air
and garden hose spray
we sweat through our clothes
down our tanned legs
our breath heavy, strong, together
not knowing
we'd do this
only one more time.
Only tonight we darted
through the dwindling numbers, up the lonely hill,
gaining speed as our bodies
settled into synchronous steps
then surged.
You stayed next to me,
feet patting the pavement when you didn't speak,
turning suddenly,
asking—
Dad, can I go on ahead?
I released my grip—
Be careful!
Watching your hair wave among
the strewn and struggling masses
turning a corner
run on and
finish ahead of me.

OUT

Changing Trains in Jamaica

From the middle of Long Island
the train ride took me
for a Broadway matinee
with my grandmother,
meeting in Jamaica,
she guiding me through
the maze of platforms for a
transfer to the subway,
in my flannel suit
hair shellacked in place
all big-boy manners and shined shoes
wobbling gently
side to side in the dark
under flickering underground lights.

I would someday say
I saw Mary Martin sing
the Hills are Alive
from the nose-bleed seats,
melodies so familiar
I already knew every note
from the album, already
loved Broadway musicals
before I knew the cliché.
I was growing into
the disparity, vaguely aware,
aching not to be,
starting to regret, to implore
please make it go away,
the birthday wish I'd repeat
for decades.

A walk to Penn Station at sunset
she kissed me on the cheek,
checked the ticket in
my pocket, left me to get
back alone—finding my way,
changing trains, pleading for
the car to jump the track.

Lingering Questions

Why didn't you seize
that momentum
on that Sunday drive—father
and son
turning a corner, coming upon
that horse, a muscled stud
beneath a green tree
heavy with summer fruit,
dandelion seedlings blowing in the air,
his apparent excitement
extending almost to his knee
demanding we not ignore him,
a stock-still tableau on a country road
staring blankly at us
through the windshield—
picture-perfect time for
the talk.
Why didn't you grasp
the reins
start the conversation,
sitting as you were
between two quivering bodies on the brink.

Why didn't you pry it out of me,
dislodge haunting questions,
my ache, the pit lodged
deep in my verdant adolescence.

Why didn't you talk to me?

Decades and decades later
and decades after your death
I still don't know but
I suspect you suspected the truth—

it was probably too late,
some words wouldn't
have changed anything,
the gate was already kicked open,
the galloping beast
unleashed, sweeping me up
into the saddle
charging away,
no one there to stop us.

The Night My Mother and I Killed a Bottle of Scotch

It's the summer when my brother comes out, creating
a category five that pummels the family walls already
cracked from the pressure of Catholic dogma, Irish
guilt, and uncontrolled procreation; this news
drives my parents well past their tolerance for disquiet,
washes away fantasies they had about a dozen
grandchildren, and sends my father to a therapist
to figure what he's done wrong.

Meanwhile my mother seeks out certainty,
decides to put an end to her suspicions about me,
resolves to steer me right before I torque in a direction
she dreads. Not both sons. She's not having it.

Can you stay for a few minutes, she says before
my foot lands on the bottom step, shredding
my plans to get out of my waiter's uniform and
meet a buddy for a midnight toke. She employs that
don't-think-about-refusing voice, and suddenly
I'm sitting on the we-should-talk-about-your-report
card couch.

I pour my first scotch, while it's clear
she's into her third at least. Before I realize it, instead
of a rubber hose, she raises her velvet pick axe, begins
to chip away, breaks through one layer at a time.
At twenty-one, I think I've spun a pretty tough
carapace but she is skilled at getting inside her children.

As I gaze over to the door, it moves away, grows smaller,
like in a Dali dream, I see my hand reach for the doorknob
as it melts. There is no escape. She reminisces about
all the girls I dated in high school, reminds me how much
fun I had, but she doesn't know I never made a move
on any of them or any girl since.

Soon I'm drunk and malleable, I am agreeing with her
about everything and admitting to her and to myself
that I really don't have a clue—about my future, about
what's standing in my way, about what I want or who
I want. There are moments in life when everything
seems crystal clear; this is not one of those moments.

The chair spins, the room spins. She is convinced
she can straighten out the road ahead by sheer
willpower. She'll rearrange the stars for me, re-order
the map if she has to. I'm too confused, too wimpy,
too guilty, too scared, to resist. I'm easy, a pushover,
and soon the bottle is empty and the bunker has caved in.

She takes the responsibility off my shoulders,
makes the decision, tells me what I'm going to do:
the cute blonde I work with at the restaurant—tomorrow,
probably badly hungover, I'll be asking her out.

The Bachelorette Party Lands in a Gay Bar

Let us roll out the red carpet for the ladies
in blue, unlatch
the gates from the inside and let them in,
a posse undeterred and undaunted.
Let a woozy woman in a temporary tiara
of little plastic penises,
squeeze in
between the barricade of our elbows.
Stand aside, everyone!
One spaghetti strap up,
one down, a single breast
about to flop out.
Let her slap down her keys
and her phone
and her beaded bag,
whack the mahogany
with a wallop.
Let her point her uncrumpled
ten into the air
like a semaphore signaling
the hordes,
This round's on me!
Let her slur *Straight up!*
as the slippery drip of gin
and Chanel drifts
up and over us.
Let a smile crack the corner
of her pale-pink lips,
her head spinning from side to side,
and let her eyes look
past us as they try to focus.
Let her think she's amazing.

We'll wait.

Reason No. 1001

(for Brad)

I hate waking up to a dishwasher
full of chaos you created last night—
moist sour air billowing out as I open
the latch & look for a clean coffee cup,
wine glasses lie horizontal, cloudy water
sloshing, dinner plates lined as close
as boot-campers, smelling the sweat
of the one in front, too close to ever
get clean, an artillery of cutlery dropped
carelessly—spoons pointing down, knives
aiming up, the melted Tupperware, victims
of a hot-air dry, expanding our carbon
footprint by inches each day. I unload
and reload, adding the detergent you forgot.

Then there's this morning when
I catch you standing in the front doorway
staring at a deer eating your roses.
An antler gone, blood across his ribs, no
doubt from a car, and your arm moves
to stop me from shooing him away. Shhh!
you say He's hurt. Let him eat. I'm reminded
of how you carried me home, wounded,
across your shoulders.

MOREOVER

It's Funny How You Remember Stuff

Seven bodies in the backseat
and another three up-front, folded in half
or wrapped around each other as only
seventeen-year-olds can manage,
we made our way from
the game to the diner, then
we crumpled ourselves again
into Mike's father's sedan,
unaware of any danger we posed
until we got pulled over
and linebacker Mike cried
his way out of a ticket,
surprising us all by confessing to the cop
his application was pending
at the Academy.

I just learned on-line he made
a career in the Navy,
married Janet, had six kids.

I never told anyone this, but I
sometimes search
the names of people
I knew before,
the people I wonder
about and who might wonder about me,
not because we were all
that close but because
it's one way to make sense
of decades
that have whooshed by,

brought us
to this peculiar place
where most of us,
according to Google,
are wrapping things up.

I Announce to an Empty Room I'm Going for a Walk

in nature, like real poets do, but I'm bored and back
in half an hour, wondering how everyone else
manages to spin gold from autumn leaves,

I return to a pile of fresh scat at my door, its
immediacy impossible to ignore.
I poke it with a stick like a TV

science person looking for clues
in the creature's diet, evidence of the doer's
entrails and identity, its motive. The scat

itself seems more important than who left it.
Sometimes our headlights catch a plump
brown fox across the road. Maybe.

I find this mystery infinitely more
engaging than pondering the falling leaves, or
the rain dirtying the window panes, or

the wide-winged buzzards above.
I try not to think of all the shit dropped,
devoid of mystery when you know who

did it, someone you knew had it in him,
so full of it he was, Larry, for five years bossing
us around to distract from his own demons.

I try a nature poem: Through the blinds,
there are trees with yellow and red prepped to dive,
wanting so much to find the earth, to be done,

turn fertilizer for acorns for someone else's future.
That's what happens when you go looking for
inspiration; you find it dead outside your door.

Be Careful

The voice returns and asks if he can
call me back—an undergrad wants help
with finding something and he's
the only one there at the moment,
says he needs to hold off on my request
in favor of the one standing in front of him.

I agree, I really have no choice, expecting
that's the end of it; he'll remember me
during the next keg party and say
omigod, I never called that guy back.

I can't drive three hours to the campus now.
After thirty-five years, I wouldn't know
where to park or how to find the archives.

But he does call back, tells me he found it,
says he scanned it and just emailed it to me.

I flip open my laptop while I am still
on the phone and click on the file.Exposed
in front of me are the forty pages I typed
on cotton paper that summer in my quiet
classroom. Pages of poems I had
forgotten, pages of who I was at thirty.
I got what I wished for.

I thank him, and he thanks me in return.
He says, I'm usually looking at algorithms
or dry histories, this was a breath of fresh
air, and hangs up.

Disproving a Negative

I'm left alone
in the examining room,
his shoes echo down
the linoleum halls,
& I snap a shot of the x-ray
lit against the wall, the compression
of time and enthusiasm—
my spine, the squishy bits
between the bones flattened
like street tar.

He returns and says, the roominess
you once felt between then and now
and the ultimate, it's all compressed.
He's not being funny.

I stare at the ceiling but can't remember
half the stuff that once excited me.

This weekend my daughter
told the story—twice—
about a litter of foxes she found
under her porch, how one of the babies
didn't make it, just wasn't there
one day. Turning fifty, she looks
at me and down
at her son who discovered
the kit was missing.

Knock, Knock, Knockin'

Entering through a side door on a
mid-week winter morning, sipping cups
of decaf & nostalgia, one after another
they hike to the lectern—recollections
of poignant first-person chronicles
(a tale of an early marriage
or a funny sketch from a grandkid's visit),
the chilly library annex thaws
in sympathetic cordiality.

Wrapping up the hour,
a left-behind folkie lovingly resurrects
a 60's song from the vault—Dylan,
of course—mumbles a brief intro and
starts strumming without naming the tune,
but they know it, heads nod to
each other, in time, memories kick in,
lips synch & toes tap softly.

But when he gets to the chorus and
motions for the group to join him,
the metronome stutters, a chill re-enters,
no one chimes in, lips lock down,
heads go still & toes come to rest
as if the wind blew open the door,
one guy stands up, turns, & shouts
will someone shut that damn thing!

Apologies to the Bus Driver Fifty Years Too Late

This never could have happened on a school bus—
there would have been consequences—but this was
a county bus, on its regular route, and we were high
school sophomores, coming home late from practice,
sitting in the back, being sophomoric, poking fun at each
other, making lewd remarks, throwing books, being jerks.
You tried to get us to calm down, you were kind, you
were firm, you were a pro, we ignored you, we insulted you,
we were private school shits and we didn't care, and
I made a point of exiting through the front door
so I could let you know how much I disdained you,
in my letter sweater, dropping down the stairs, giving
you my final swipe, No wonder you're a bus driver.

Tied

My father taught me to tie a Windsor knot and today I am sure I can remember even though it's been years, but I try twice, and each time the tying feels right and looks right but the tie turns out exactly backwards. You offer to help but for some reason I can't explain I don't want another person's hands on me today, and I suspect you won't know how and will get pissed at me instead of at yourself. You ask me often how I am, watch me carefully when I stand up from my chair, so sure I am going to careen face-first into a wall or bang my head on the edge of the bed. I'm sure this spread collar will look peculiar if I just tie a regular knot but that's what I wind up doing. I forgot to put in the stays before I buttoned up so you will have to put your hands near my throat anyway to push them where they belong and when we are both done, and ready to go to the wedding of the neighbor's kid I've never even met, you get a look in your eye, on your whole face, and say you look so handsome and I realize how much I needed to hear that again.

The Load Uncarried

If you've ever had
a wooden clothes hanger
broken, cracked
across your back as you
ran from your mother
who was trying
to sleep it off on a Saturday morning,

or ever spanked your child,

consider now, the full house still
in bed, my daughter holds
her toddler son who cried
himself into hysterics—
can't stop, gasps for air—
& whispers soothing words
into his matted hair
his salty face,
for half an hour until he stops
the hiccups, shudders and goes
limp in her arms,

then you might see the circle—
the chase around the house
down the hall
through the kitchen
through the dining room
the living room
back down the hall
past her bedroom—
that circle has been broken,
and sense the weight,

the dense leftover sting
on your shoulders,
is maybe
gone for good.

These Houses Are Too Close

The screen porch frames our neighbor
in hazy mid-morning half-light,
bald head rising above gray couch,
he faces a dried-out herb garden, grips
the coffee he made himself,
leans back, away from the day ahead
as if he sees something we can't.
He's aware he wanes,
but he's here—the older one, and
unprepared.

Later he lobs
a hint across the fence as we shake
our summer cocktails. We relent,
help him cross the uneven lawn,
nod again when he asks again,
"Did you know that Helen died."
We don't need, don't want
to be reminded.

We've signed papers,
memorized passwords, decided
what the grandkids get of what's left from
our wild living, your hair goes
early gray,
my beard pokes out in spikey tufts,
we turn the twisty thing to save
the bread. Someone has to go first
if a crash won't settle it &
take us both out at once.
Tonight while you're away
on business,
I'll make too much lasagna.

The future is a magician
in drag wearing a bad wig.

Discovery

On this cloud-covered day when we stay
home from the beach, I am sitting on the slate

grey patio watching my two grandsons hunched
over something at the edge of the garden.

They have a new toy—a magnifying glass
I gave them, and they are poring over a world

I can't see from here. All I hear is there and try
that one and yee-ow and this here. They are

seeing the world for themselves, insects
& others, innocent forms of flora and fauna—

all looking fresh and new to their little eyes,
and then the sun pokes through enough to

shine a beam. I hear them scream
with delight as they fry some thing to a crisp.

OTHER

A Poetic Biography

I'm reading the on-line biography of a famous
writer, a laureate, one whose language
is so clever it makes me quake,
whose life in academia hovers in the background,
the life of I-have-time-and-space-to-write.
We are both old men now, but
it says that he was born
a few years before me, and I think
"Oh, good. I still have time."

Then I click on a video where he twangs
so matter-of-factly about himself and
his writing and quaintly blathers about failing and
failing again and I take heart until
I see his country porch on his country house
off a mud dried road and then
just to make me feel worse
he puts a floppy mushroom hat
and plucks a goddam banjo for heaven's sake.
At least he's not wearing overalls
doesn't remove his teeth.
In a close-up I notice his moustache needs a trim
his wire-rim eye glasses are slightly askew
explaining his view of the world.
How did those crags get carved into his face?

So I go outside and add chlorine to the pool
and take a long swim to clear my head.

Ada Limon Perches on My Knee and Reads Her Poems

The PBS station on mute tonight,
a ballet comes into focus,
my smart phone in front of me, I scroll
through the nonsense, land abruptly
on a live link to her inaugural poetry
reading in our nation's library, I planned
to go before this damn hurricane decided to stay.

I flip the rectangular phone
on its side, a landscape view of dazzling
blood-red dress and streaming cinnamon hair,
prop her up, settle her on my knee.
I press volume, lyrics ascend through
the floorboards of the silent hall,
of the hushed on-line audience,
the marble-lined tunnels of Congress.

She moves fluidly through windy pages
on the podium, the ballet
twirls on my wall, forms a backdrop
of whirling limbs leaping across my living room—
a larger-than-life dance backdropping
a poet in my hand, her voice drops
melting ice cubes in a lake, circles
of fearlessness ripple from the center,
her smiling delivery is everything I need
tonight, shrinking me to human size
in amazement of human agility, in awe.

I recall the day my breathing stopped:
Can the words on this page be doing this?
Dumbstruck & finally managing
to raise my hand, asked if what I think
I just saw was real, and the professor
smiled and said, Yes, that's art.

Hamartia

The four of us back in the car heading to a
West Virginia weekend, they make me
defend my actions—or inaction actually—
when the waitress back there got snippy
with me, gave me some good-natured lip
because I couldn't decide on a condiment,
I explain to my too-thoughtful fellows how
the bop on the head she gave me hardly hurt
was in good fun and she reminded me

of the salty gals back on Long Island,
the ones I worked with in my teens, them serving
and me clearing, where I got a different schooling,
said I rather enjoyed her refreshing sharpness
tired as I was of the mayonnaise life in D.C.
but after a few minutes explaining
I wonder if they have a point.

We cross the mountains & fall foliage
meanders me back to the autumn day
I took a black eye from the town bully,
just stood there straddling the bike seat
while his thighs held the front tire still,
left me to explain the stain, to consider lessons
I could've got that day, how life would come
at me like a raised fist and how I should've
learned to box.

Once Again, the Flock

Dawn, I lean over the steering wheel, look up.
Traveling, linked invisibly against a grey sky
their outline expanding like a spill
shifting their positions
coupled for life, moving, a still autumn journey.
October, the Chesapeake landscape dim and dull,
a flock above my head, honking
above the harvested fields, corn stalks lie down
against the new chill, brown remnants withered,
like an exhausted traveler collapsing in the dust.

Noon, forty cycles later, I return, drive
the same roads, a few miles and messy tears
from that life, to the route,
watching again these geese gliding overhead.
I quickly close the car windows
to keep the blown leaves out,
heading home, to an aging man's dry bed.
I peer above the wheel again,
again descendants spreading wide against
a feathery cloud, the same fixed and moving form
I saw then,
in constancy they reiterate.

Dusk, I park beside the fresh sod lawn,
enter a house bathed in falling down shadows
unpack the moving crate—the hallway clock
and hunt for the winding key into the night.

The next morning, swooping over the roof,
not leaving—the warmer days keep them close—
they consider moving on, but don't.

SAD

There's just enough sun for us to set sail
against a backdrop of blackberry clouds

moving—at least we hope they're moving—
away from us down the coast, while

we hurriedly tack west towards open sea, late
afternoon, the short edge of evening, night

right behind, sleep threatening to overtake us
& pull the shades before we're ready.

Lately I remember these dreams, they disturb
my sleep even if the details don't stick.

I wake up floating towards an open door
in the sky. September used to usher in a panic,

I'd see its shadows elongate, whisper dark
murmurings about how gloom would assume

the helm in January, I'd do things I was too scared
to do the rest of the year, like tell lies

about where I was last night. Take heart, screw
your courage to the sticking place, I'd tell myself

while the door would swing shut on autumn
hinges, before I knew what was coming.

The History of Rock & Roll

The all-night drive opens in pieces—
three-minute bites and 60's songs
streamed from above, a chasing satellite

a silver-tipped beam tracked our veering
path (escaping the plague) and kept us in sight.
After we argued for three days over

the definition of an underlying condition.
Should we try to get home while we can?
Songs in the dark, do you know this one too?

I half-hummed a few lyrics
remembered hits from before you were born,
I tried to explain

what "doo-wop" was. Noises
off, so here I could collapse into
a metaphor about depths, a pitch road

ahead, shallow-breathing, shadows falling
across the globe. An hour of silence, no
singing, the pavement buzz beneath us,

the pressure expanded, threatening to burst
like an over-filled tire. Did your mind
roll into a muddy ditch like mine did

& did you lay there wondering what if?
Then you found the 50's station,
asked how Patti Page became Chuck Berry,

asked, how did everything get so different.

Pandemic Blues Day 43: In Which I Invite the Germs In

I busy myself making
sourdough starter,
involving ingredients I don't have
to shop for—flour and water, and hope
a few sympathetic microbes will fly
into my kitchen alive and ready to work,
leaven this flat feeling that our lockdown
could last what's left of my life. I'm doing whatever
keeps me from sleeping
all day, drinking too much.
On YouTube the helpful man uses just
a measuring cup, eschews
a digital scale and all its romantic precision.
Just eyeball it, leave something to chance he says.
This recipe for anarchy, his casual approach
suits me fine. I think of all the things
you can do just enough—

like a life—chug along for years without a plan,
dump tinker toys onto the carpet
knowing a few pieces are lost,
make what you can
or take a road trip in an old car
with squiggly-line signs to warn you
of the cliff, but not when you'll meet it.
A carefree journey marked
by ambiguous symbology, open to interpretation
open to hope—

So when the gloppy mess goes rancid after a few days
I pour it down the drain, mix a new batch of chaos,
lid the jar loosely, open a window,
welcome the air from outside, hope
for a different outcome.

How to Draw a Line Without a Pencil

No more the cycles we spun through,
dinners we laughed through,
no hunting, no gathering. What a wingman
you were! Sunday waking to your dawn calls for help—
your car keys lost somewhere in the night,
your phone stolen by someone you fell for.

We were late arrivers then, nearly fifty. Life
re-opening, mine like a ski slope,
yours a cathedral window,
convinced we'd caught the updraft
soaring, rose-colored clouds
edges singed by the flames we'd seen.

Here tonight in your house on
the hill, up from the shimmering bay,
a sailboat's dark triangle against
a blazing autumn sun, slipping quietly,
your eyes hollowed out now
by pain you're trying to hide,
the machine you need
in your bedroom out of sight.

You speak of a childhood friend
I picture how that call went—
you desperate for another flight,
a sixty-year-old donor better than none,
gambling outdoes certainty when certainty
is unthinkable—
did you have to beg?

We both get quiet, I stare
at the silence melting in my glass, we're both
relieved you never called me, never put
me on the spot, placed a chip there.
Over your shoulder the light drops
beneath the blue-black horizon. I want
to say thank you, but how would
that sound?

The President Signs the Criminal Justice Reform Act

In the Oval Office adorned in rehearsed applause
from the full-pocketed and the bloated,
paid to do a job by corporate wardens enriched
by a three-strike law that scooped up traffic
violators like escaped farm animals,

surrounded by billionaire brothers who bought
a conscience on closeout, after years of dictating to
lap dog stenographers in the Capitol their wishes,
placing innocents into the jaws of a meat grinder,

smoothing silk tie with one hand he grins
and turns with camera-ready graciousness to his left
to his right, cloaks himself in the mantle of
unearned praise, halfway extends his barely average
hands to his greedy kin who get credit for
finally noticing injustice because now
it nested in their family patch,

he moves the pen up and down with theatrical force,
forging a scribbled signature, turning his name towards
the cameras like a child with a finger painting.

I watch this revival-tent duplicity on my TV,
wondering, how do we mend a wingless sparrow, how
do we put a daddy's push on the seat of a girl's swing, how
do we place a mother's palm on a boy's delicate
fingers guiding as he practices his letters?

How will a new law fix a bad law, return
the confiscated, lift all the clothes and furniture
evicted to the curb and fly them back inside the house?

This Flag Is Not Waving

move the weights   add ten more pounds   pull down
the bar on the lat machine   notice
the ginger swinging
free weights like tinker toys
Did I leave the eggs boiling over the flame
again   they end up
with burn marks and their shells smell
like chalk   the crane through the window lowered
a stack of I-beams to the ground
sister wrote the assignment on the board
this town has outgrown its original
intent   the gunman had no trouble
my driver's license expires the same month
as my car and they want me
to take a test so I can prove I still have
it   I think I might move
across the room   to the barbells and
how the bench still has his sweat on it
his shorts are so thick   we need more
propane for tonight's steaks
It's not the same country I grew up in, California
fires won't be extinguished no
matter how long the hoses
how good the chemicals
pill this morning   people don't wipe
up their sweat   expect others to   so I hold
the door open as I exit   for the person
behind me I can't see but just
sense is there   sensitive like my mother
said I was
I didn't know what she meant
but now I get it.

We Promised

We boomed and we banged
We lay down in the streets and held high our signs
and declared the world saved by our purity of purpose
by our childhood, our hair.
We rocked and we trolled
traipsed naked over the fields
with melodies
rising behind us
and we watched our brothers die
from disease and in
crusades that our deciders
triggered and discounted.
Then we discarded our used
needles and bibles,
we popped a pill
paid the piper and the banker and the doctor.
We told our children to shake hands after they lost
to bring canned goods to school
said it didn't matter what tribe
walked through the door for dinner
and we meant it
for a time
and then went back to the laundry
and our golf swings,
we mounted our stationary bicycles
and gave away our daughters and buried our sons
in foreign darkness and dust storms,
again we said prayers
to heal that poor kid on TV in the bombed out house
we dusted the furniture
we stopped
carrying each other off the field
and we held up the foundations that held up the world.

We grew old in our new clothes
we bypassed our hearts' beatings and
stared at the grocery bags in our clenched hands
We said we voted and didn't, or did
for all we once despised
gave up, gave in
we said no
we said we are better than that
and we won't sanction that
and finally
we had to admit
we lied.

About the Author

Jack Mackey holds a master's degree in English from the University of Maryland and was awarded a fellowship in poetry from the Delaware Division of the Arts. Jack is an active member in local writer's organizations including Coastal Writers, Rehoboth Beach Writer's Guild, and the Eastern Shore Writer's Association. His poetry has been published in a variety of literary journals including *Gargoyle, Third Wednesday, Broadkill Review, Anti Heroin Chic,* and *Panoply.* Jack divides his time between Delaware, South Florida, and Lisbon, Portugal.

His website is:
www.jackmackeypoet.com

www.ingramcontent.com/pod-product-compliance
Lightning Source LLC
Chambersburg PA
CBHW022015160426
43197CB00007B/448